PEOPLE WHO MADE HISTORY IN
ANCIENT ROME

by Patricia Levy
Illustrated by Richard Hook

HODDER
Wayland

an imprint of Hodder Children's Books

Produced for Hodder Wayland by
White-Thomson Publishing Ltd
2/3 St. Andrew's Place
Lewes
BN7 1UP

People who made history in

Ancient Greece • Ancient Egypt • Ancient Rome • Native Americans

Series concept: Alex Woolf
Editor: Susan Behar
Consultant: Dr Philip de Souza, Lecturer in Classical Studies,
   St Mary's University College, Twickenham
Picture research: Shelley Noronha
Cover design: Jan Sterling
Inside design: Stonecastle Graphics Ltd
Map artwork: Peter Bull

Published in Great Britain in 2000 by Hodder Wayland, a division of
Hodder Children's Books.
This edition published in 2001.

A Catalogue record for this book is available from the British Library.

ISBN 07502 3262 5

Printed and bound in G. Canale & C. S.p.A. - Borgaro T.se (Turin)

Hodder Children's Books
A division of Hodder Headline Limited
338 Euston Road, London NW1 3BH

Picture acknowledgements
The publisher would like to
thank the following for their
kind permission to use these
pictures: AKG Photo 4, 13, 18, 25,
34, 41; The Bridgeman Art
Library 12, 16, 20, 21, 25, 29;
British Museum 14, 24; C M
Dixon 8, 22, 36; e.t. archive 10,
17, 28, 30, 33, 37, 38, 40, 42;
Michael Holford 26, 32, 43; Tony
Stone/Richard Elliott 5; Werner
Forman Archive 6, 9

Contents

Who were the ancient Romans?

ROME'S POWER grew gradually over several hundred years, until the Roman Empire at its height, in the time of the emperor Trajan (AD 98–117), extended from modern Portugal in the west to Britain in the far north to Mesopotamia in the east and Egypt in the south.

Throughout its history, Rome fought many wars with its neighbours. These wars helped to make Rome rich in booty, slaves and taxes taken from its defeated enemies.

▲ A marble carving showing a butcher at work in his shop. He has a block cleaver, similar to those used by modern butchers, and has hung pieces of meat around the shop.

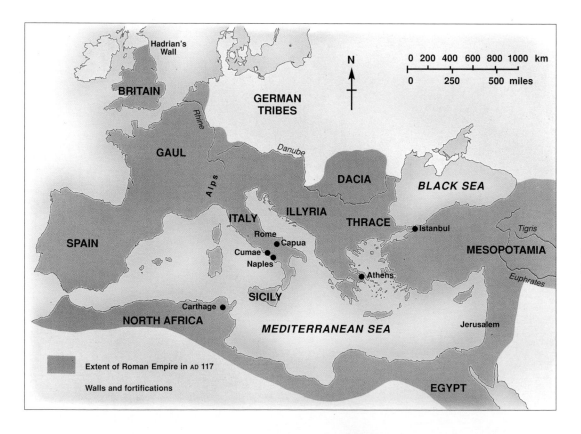

◄ The Roman Empire at its height in the second century AD.

The empire also depended heavily on trade. From Dacia (modern Romania) and Spain came gold and silver, Spain and North Africa provided horses, and grain – a very important food – came from all over the empire.

The Roman people worked in a variety of jobs, much like people today. They were lawyers, teachers, craftsmen, builders, priests, soldiers, writers, shopkeepers, merchants, sailors and firemen. The wealthy lived in both the town and the countryside, and many had farms worked by tenants and slaves. Unlike their rich employers, the tenants lived in simple houses and farmed the land. In the cities, people lived in six-storey blocks of flats, ate in restaurants, drew water from the city's plumbing system, used public communal flushing toilets, visited the baths daily and attended massive amphitheatres where they watched plays, or fights to the death between slaves, known as the 'games'. The wealthy lived very easy lives, usually relaxing in the afternoons, while slaves did most of the hard work.

▲ The Colosseum, dedicated in AD 80. It measured 200 metres long and 150 metres wide and could hold up to 45,000 spectators, who watched games involving fights to the death between gladiators (including women) and wild beasts.

ROMAN JUSTICE

The Roman view of justice and punishment was very different from our own. There was no police force apart from the magistrates and their few assistants, and they had no power to investigate or arrest as our police do. There were also no prison guards or prisons. Instead, people were punished by fines, exile, being forced into slavery, sent to fight at the games, or by being flogged or executed.

Ancient Rome in the time of Tarquin

IN ABOUT 753 BC, a group of villages arranged on seven hills formed a single community that came to be known as Rome, and which later became the capital city and centre of the Roman Empire. Rome developed on an important crossing point on the river Tiber, which meant that it had plenty of contact with neigbouring cultures such as the Greeks and Etruscans and was a centre of communication.

Rome was ruled by kings, chosen by the Senate, an advisory council to the king, made up of wealthy nobles. The king was very powerful; he made the laws, acted as a judge, controlled building projects in the growing city, as well as being in charge of the army. The nobles contributed wealth to the state, fought in the army when needed, and made sure that their followers were loyal to the king. Between 753 and 510 BC Roman historians tell us that seven kings ruled Rome. The last, and worst, of them was Tarquin.

▼ Roman culture was influenced by Etruscan civilization. In this ivory carving of a banquet, two Etruscans are almost lying down as they eat at a low table, just as the Romans were to do later.

TARQUIN

**King of Rome
sixth century BC**

The stories surrounding Tarquin's rule in Rome say that he was a strong but heartless tyrant who drove the people of Rome into hard, unpaid labour on his many building projects. According to legend, after a woman called Lucretia was assaulted by one of Tarquin's sons, the people of Rome rose in rebellion against Tarquin's harsh rule. At the time, Tarquin was fighting a war against another city, and when he heard the news he rushed back to Rome to re-establish his rule, but it was too late. The citizens had shut the gates of the city against him and declared that Rome would never have another king. Instead, the nobles ruled Rome as a republic.

MYTH OR TRUTH?

Although the stories about Tarquin's cruelty and tyrannical behaviour come from the ancient Roman historians, some modern historians think that they are really myths created to justify the overthrow of Tarquin. The historians had to explain why a great king who created beautiful buildings was overthrown and how the kingdom became a republic ruled by nobles.

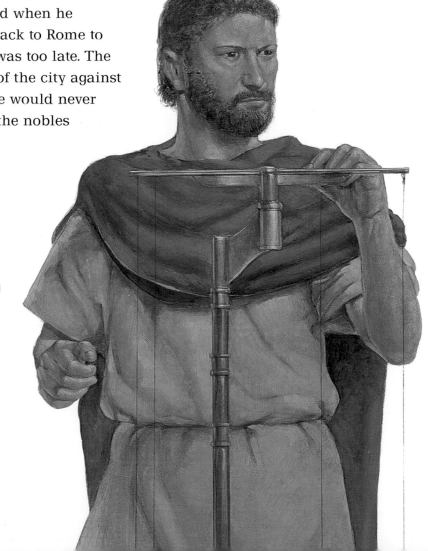

► Tarquin depicted with a groma, an instrument used by Roman land surveyors to obtain straight lines and right-angles. During Tarquin's reign in Rome he initiated many public building projects.

SPOTLIGHT ON TARQUIN

Name:	Tarquinius Superbus
Born:	Sixth century BC
Died:	In exile in southern Italy
Family:	Grandfather was the king of Rome
	He had two sons and a daughter
Most important act:	Peace treaty with Gabii, a town 19 km east of Rome
Personality:	Bossy, arrogant, shameless
Best moment:	Completing the temple to Jupiter, Juno and Minerva in Rome
Worst moment:	Being shut out of Rome

Tarquin's Fight for Rome

Tarquin was a very stubborn man. When he was shut out of Rome, he persuaded the rulers of other Italian city states to invade. Their armies were beaten, but, undeterred, Tarquin went to Clusium, another powerful city state, to ask its king for help. In 508 BC Rome was besieged by the ruler of Clusium, Lars Porsena, who was so impressed by the bravery of the Romans that he withdrew. Tarquin still didn't give up and persuaded another Latin ruler to attack in 499 BC. This also failed and Tarquin finally had to admit defeat. He fled into exile in Cumae in southern Italy, where he later died.

▶ Tarquin built a temple to the important Roman god Jupiter and goddesses Juno and Minerva. This statue represents Minerva, the goddess of wisdom, healing and arts.

THE SYBIL OF CUMAE

There is a story that Tarquin was once offered a set of nine books of prophecies by the Sybil of Cumae, a very important priestess who could tell the future. He refused to pay the price she wanted for these books, thinking that she would lower her demands, but, instead, she threw three of them onto a fire. Then she offered the remaining six books to him at the same price and he refused again, this time thinking that six was a bad bargain when he could have had nine. So she threw three more on to the fire. Finally he saw how important the books were and gave her the price she had originally asked.

▼ The cave where the sybil of Cumae is believed to have lived. Sybils were Greek prophetesses, chiefly of the god Apollo, who would go into a trance and deliver the words of the god to the people who came to ask for help.

Ancient Rome in the time of Spartacus

BY 100 BC the Roman world included most of the Mediterranean coastline and southern France. With every new territory came more slaves. It was by using slave labour that the Romans were able to build and maintain beautiful buildings, roads, aqueducts and sewers.

Slaves were thought of as property, to be owned by their masters. Whilst wealthy Romans lived lives of idleness, troops of slaves, sometimes as many as 400, catered to their every need. In some jobs, such as mining, it was cheaper to work slaves to death rather than feed them and keep them healthy. A beautiful or talented slave could cost as much as a luxury car might today, while an ugly or talentless one might cost as little as a second-hand computer. However, slaves could buy their freedom or their owners could grant it, and some ex-slaves became famous or rich.

▼ At the games, slaves were forced to fight to the death with wild animals or against one another. Those who were reluctant to fight were prodded with hot irons.

SPARTACUS

**Bandit
circa 100 BC**

We know very little about Spartacus' private life before he became famous. He was from Thrace, a country outside Roman rule with a reputation as a wild place and inhabited by fierce warriors. Thrace and Rome often fought, and it was perhaps during one of these conflicts that Spartacus joined, or was conscripted into, the Roman army.

GLADIATORIAL SCHOOLS

Strong and fit male slaves were often chosen as fighters in gladiatorial contests. They were trained in special schools and then sent to fight other slaves in front of large Roman audiences in the amphitheatres. These fights were very different to the boxing or wrestling matches of today as the gladiators were expected to fight to the death.

Perhaps he didn't like the conditions or couldn't face years of fighting, but for some reason he deserted from the army and became a bandit, raiding Roman settlements and living in the hills. Eventually, he was captured and taken to a gladiatorial school at Capua to train as a gladiator. Thracian slaves were given a round shield and a dagger to fight with and were often set against much better armed fighters. As a gladiator, he faced certain death in combat once he had finished training.

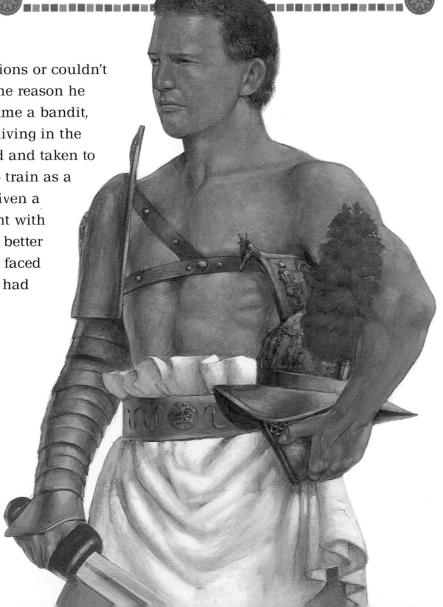

▶ As a conscript, Spartacus would have been committed to many years service in the Roman army.

SPOTLIGHT ON SPARTACUS

Name:	Spartacus
Born:	Unknown date, Thrace
Died:	On the battlefield, Lucania, 71 BC
Family:	Unknown
Special skills:	A natural leader
Personality:	Competent, brave and humane
Best moment:	Leading his troops against powerful Roman armies
Worst moment:	Deciding to return to Italy instead of fleeing into Gaul

The Slave Revolt

Spartacus led a revolt of about 70 slaves in the gladiator school in Capua in 73 BC. The runaway slaves hid in the wild on Mount Vesuvius. Other runaway slaves, originally from Gaul, Spain and Germany, joined them, and soon Spartacus commanded an army of thousands. After a time their numbers reached 90,000. Spartacus led his troops northwards, devastating towns in southern Italy on the way. Three separate Roman armies were sent to fight against them — all were defeated.

▶ A relief carving of slaves, captured by the Romans, being led away in chains.

Eventually, Spartacus led his slaves to Gaul, where he hoped they would return to their countries of origin or lose themselves in the countryside. But the slaves wanted to continue to fight, so Spartacus decided to lead them southwards. He planned to make his way to Sicily, perhaps to hold the island against the Romans, but the pirate ships he depended on failed to show up. Eight Roman legions were sent against him.

Unfortunately for Spartacus, they were commanded by Crassus, one of the most powerful men in Rome. The slave army scattered and was beaten by the superior Roman troops. Spartacus was finally killed on the battlefield, fighting to the last, even though he knew he was beaten.

▲ Spartacus and his troops would have faced a fierce Roman army armed with shields and powerful weapons (as depicted here), while his men were runaways who only had whatever weapons and armour they could steal.

CRUEL CRASSUS

Unlike Spartacus, Crassus was cruel, untrustworthy and motivated solely by greed. He made much of his fortune by buying and selling slaves. He feared that if the slaves were not punished horribly then other slaves, who greatly outnumbered Roman citizens, might also rebel. He had 6,000 captured slaves crucified along the road from Rome to Capua, where the rebellion had begun.

Ancient Rome
in the time of Julius Caesar

BY 264 BC, the Republic of Rome had come to dominate all of Italy. In 201 BC, it had defeated the powerful state of Carthage in North Africa, and so became the most important place in the Mediterranean.

For 400 years after the expulsion of Tarquin, Rome was governed as a republic by a group of senators. Over this period, the republic grew to be powerful but corrupt. The nobility were interested mainly in becoming rich by taking loot and slaves from conquered territories. While the nobility benefited, the poor people resented having to fight in wars from which they did not profit. Peasants who owned small farms had to compete with the big landowners who used slaves to farm their large estates. It was these peasants who supported a successful soldier, called Julius Caesar, when he fought to take control of Rome.

► Julius Caesar led a successful nine-year campaign against Gaul. This coin depicts prisoners from Gaul and bears his name. It was probably made to celebrate his achievements in war.

JULIUS CAESAR
Dictator
circa 100–44 BC

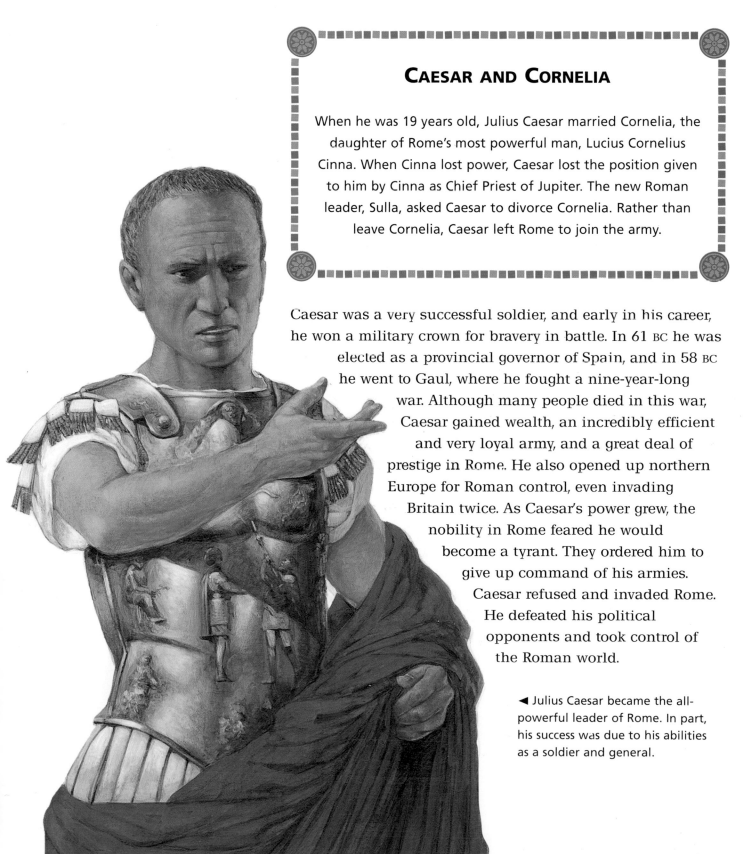

CAESAR AND CORNELIA

When he was 19 years old, Julius Caesar married Cornelia, the daughter of Rome's most powerful man, Lucius Cornelius Cinna. When Cinna lost power, Caesar lost the position given to him by Cinna as Chief Priest of Jupiter. The new Roman leader, Sulla, asked Caesar to divorce Cornelia. Rather than leave Cornelia, Caesar left Rome to join the army.

Caesar was a very successful soldier, and early in his career, he won a military crown for bravery in battle. In 61 BC he was elected as a provincial governor of Spain, and in 58 BC he went to Gaul, where he fought a nine-year-long war. Although many people died in this war, Caesar gained wealth, an incredibly efficient and very loyal army, and a great deal of prestige in Rome. He also opened up northern Europe for Roman control, even invading Britain twice. As Caesar's power grew, the nobility in Rome feared he would become a tyrant. They ordered him to give up command of his armies. Caesar refused and invaded Rome. He defeated his political opponents and took control of the Roman world.

◄ Julius Caesar became the all-powerful leader of Rome. In part, his success was due to his abilities as a soldier and general.

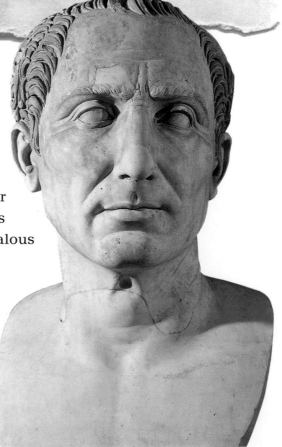

SPOTLIGHT ON JULIUS CAESAR

Name:	Gaius Julius Caesar
Born:	July 12th 100 BC
Died:	Knife wounds, 15th March 44 BC
Family:	Roman nobility
Married:	1. Cornelia 2. Pompeia 3. Calpurnia
Children:	Julia, daughter of Cornelia, Caesarion, son of Queen Cleopatra of Egypt
Personality:	Strong-willed, ambitious, never bore a grudge, charismatic
Worst moment:	Stabbed by his friend Brutus
Last words:	Et tu, Brute ('and you, Brutus')
Most famous words:	Veni, vidi, vici ('I came, I saw, I conquered', after winning a battle in Turkey)

Caesar in Power

Caesar ruled Rome for several years, from 49–44 BC. During this time, he carried out very important reforms. For example, he changed the calendar, cancelled debts caused by the war, and rewarded his troops with land. These reforms made him very popular with the troops and ordinary people. Unfortunately, this led to his downfall. In 44 BC, he was assassinated by jealous noblemen who feared his power. His death led to more bloodshed in Rome and the rise to power of his heir, Augustus Caesar.

▶ Although Julius Caesar rejected the title of king, he had himself made into a god just before his death.

CAESAR OUTWITS THE PIRATES

In 75 BC Caesar was captured by pirates who demanded a ransom of 20 talents. Caesar told them to make the ransom higher, arguing that the sum was too small for such an important man. When the money arrived, Caesar was released. He raised a fleet of ships and went back to the island where he had been held captive. He had the pirates captured and crucified and took back the ransom money, plus all the pirates' loot.

Julius Caesar's downfall came about because he tried to carry out too many reforms too quickly. But his legacy to Rome is that he made it possible for his heirs to have absolute power, paving the way for the rule of the emperors.

◄ This mosaic depicts a Roman garrison by the river Nile in Egypt. In 48 BC Julius Caesar and his troops entered Egypt, where he fell in love with Cleopatra, whom he made Queen of Egypt.

Ancient Rome in the time of Virgil

WRITERS WERE quite important figures in Roman society and a great deal of the information that we now have about ancient Rome comes from their surviving works. Julius Caesar himself wrote careful accounts of his various campaigns, and some poor men found that they could become wealthy and respected through writing.

Rome's first public library was opened sometime during Augustus' reign but, before that, there were bookshops selling 10-metre long parchment scrolls that were to be read aloud. Plays were an important part of Roman life, although not as important as the games, and several successful playwrights began their lives as slaves or the sons of freedmen.

► This wall painting shows actors performing in a play. Romans loved to go to the theatre to see comedies and tragedies, and some of these survive to the present day.

VIRGIL
Poet
circa 70–19 BC

Virgil was the most influential and successful poet of ancient Rome. He grew up while Julius Caesar was struggling for power in Rome, and later he saw more civil wars during the rise of Augustus Caesar. Later, Augustus established his power and life in Rome became peaceful and prosperous for its citizens. After so many years of civil war, Virgil's poetry is full of the hatred of such wars and the harm that they do to the state.

Virgil's family were ordinary Roman citizens. When his father inherited a farm, he was able to pay to have Virgil educated, an important step in helping Virgil to gain social status in Rome. Virgil spent several years studying rhetoric, medicine, astronomy and philosophy. He discovered his brilliant talent for poetry in his late teens.

> ## PATRONAGE IN ANCIENT ROME
>
> At first, a person who wanted to be a writer depended on getting the interest of a rich man, known as patronage. This can be seen in some poetry or stories where a writer praises a particular man. But, once established, they were independent of their sponsors and could write more honestly.

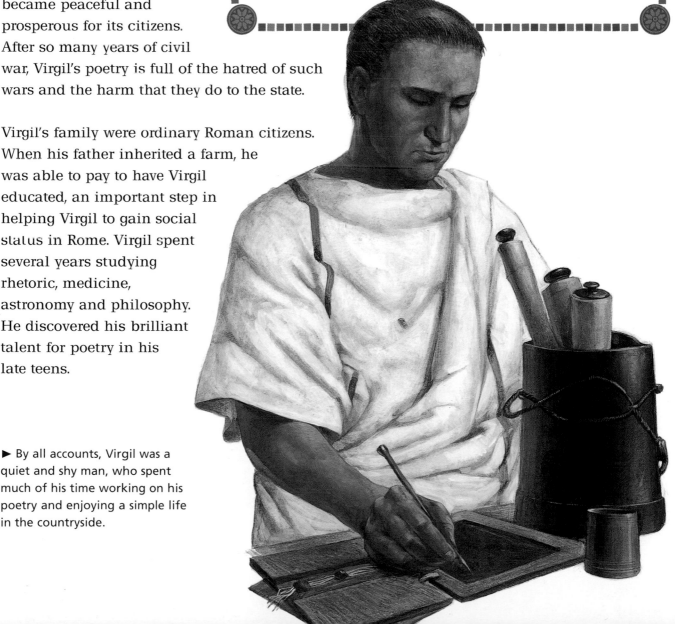

▶ By all accounts, Virgil was a quiet and shy man, who spent much of his time working on his poetry and enjoying a simple life in the countryside.

SPOTLIGHT ON VIRGIL

Name:	Publius Virgil Maro
Born:	70 BC near Mantua, Cisalpine, Gaul
Family:	His father may have owned a pottery. He inherited a farm, where he kept bees
Married:	No
Education:	Studied in Milan, Naples and Rome
Appearance:	Tall, sturdily built, dark haired, rustic
Personality:	Very modest, shy
Best moment:	Reading verses of his poem the *Aeneid* aloud to Augustus Caesar
Worst moment:	Having his farm confiscated in 42 BC and given to Roman soldiers

Virgil's Poetry

Virgil was a shy man, never married and took no part in politics. His earliest poetry is about his love of the countryside and the old values of Rome, such as religion. He was recognized as a good poet and made friends with Augustus Caesar, who asked him to write a poem about Rome. The result, which took Virgil ten years to write, was the narrative poem, the *Aeneid,* about the early history of Rome. The *Aeneid* is still studied in schools and universities today. It has influenced Roman and English writers down through the centuries.

► For hundreds of years Virgil has been admired as a great poet. This marble statue of him was made in the 13th century for a cathedral in Mantua in Italy.

THE ELDER AND YOUNGER PLINY

There were two famous ancient Roman writers called Elder and Younger Pliny. Elder Pliny commanded the Roman fleet on the Bay of Naples and died in the eruption of the volcano Vesuvius in AD 79. He wrote an encyclopaedia called the *Natural World*, which was all about human achievements, not about natural history. His nephew and adopted son Younger Pliny was a senator, and he is best known for his *Letters* and a long speech he wrote in praise of the Emperor Trajan. It is through the works of writers like Elder and Younger Pliny that we know about the ancient Romans.

▼ A fourth century pavement from Somerset, England, illustrates events from the *Aeneid*. We can see the ships of the hero Aeneas arriving from Africa, and the meeting of Dido, queen of Carthage (in north Africa), with Aeneas.

In 19 BC Virgil had finished the rough draft of his great poem, the *Aeneid*, and he set off on a tour of Greece. He intended to polish up his poem and then retire to study philosophy. On his way he met Augustus at Athens. Augustus persuaded him instead to go back to Rome with him, but on the way he caught a fever and died at Brundisium. He was buried in a tomb on the road to Naples. In his will he asked that the *Aeneid* be burned but, thankfully for the millions of people who have read and appreciated his poem since, his friends ignored his request.

Ancient Rome in the time of Julia Augusta

AFTER THE murder of Julius Caesar, Rome was thrown into civil war as various groups of nobles fought to take control. Eventually, Julius Caesar's great nephew, Augustus, took power in 27 BC. He liked to be called *princeps*, which means 'leading noble'. He ruled for 41 years and was very powerful. His wife Julia Augusta became a very wealthy and influential member of Roman society.

At this time, women had few rights. Only a small number owned property or money, and no woman, rich or poor, could take part in elections. They were free, however, to go to the marketplace, the public baths and the theatre. Almost every woman had a guardian — either her husband, father or even her son. Whilst women from rich families supervised the household slaves and had large families, poorer women had to work. For example, they may have run market stalls or shops.

Marriage was very important to rich families, and they were always arranged. The daughter of one important family would marry the son of another and in that way the two families would be even wealthier.

► Weathy Roman women organized the household slaves, who did all the chores, such as cooking and cleaning.

JULIA AUGUSTA

Wife of the Emperor circa 58 BC—AD 29

SHRINE TO CONCORDIA

Augustus built many of Rome's finest buildings when he was in power. After his death, Julia Augusta became interested in public building works. One building that she personally paid for was the Shrine to Concordia. It stood in the middle of a public walkway, or portico, which was also built by her. The building was set in magnificent gardens and contained many paintings by famous artists.

The way for a woman to become powerful was to marry a powerful man. Julia Augusta became very powerful because she married the Emperor Augustus. She married her first husband when she was about 15 and she had two sons but, while she was still pregnant with the second, Augustus fell in love with her. Her first husband divorced her but still attended her wedding to Augustus.

▶ Although many of Julia Augusta's portraits depict her as a loyal and faithful wife and a good mother, she was also known as a successful hostess, who entertained Romans who wanted help and support from her husband, the Emperor Augustus.

SPOTLIGHT ON JULIA AUGUSTA

Given name:	Livia
Official name:	Julia Augusta
Born:	58 BC
Died:	AD 29, aged 86
Family:	Roman nobility
Married:	1. Tiberius Claudius Nero, 42 BC, aged 15
	2. Augustus Caesar, 39 BC
Personality:	Modest, hard working, public spirited, loyal, some say scheming
Best moment:	Made into a goddess after her death
Worst moment:	Death of her favourite son, Drusus

Julia's Augusta's Influence

As wife of the emperor, Julia Augusta owned both money and property. She bought a house that was beautifully decorated, and invited powerful men for dinner parties. People would visit her to ask for favours because they thought she could persuade Augustus to do what she wanted.

When Augustus died, he was made a god, and Julia Augusta was made the high priestess of his temple. It was at this time that she was given the name Julia Augusta. Her real name was Livia Drusilla.

► Augustus was very attached to his wife and listened to her advice. He promoted the idea of large families, although he had only one surviving daughter.

Some Roman historians believed that Julia Augusta plotted to have Tiberius, her son from her first marriage, adopted by Augustus, so that he could be the next ruler of Rome, and that she had all other possible heirs killed. Julia and Augustus had no surviving children, so Augustus made Tiberius his heir.

▼ Like many wealthy Roman women, Julia Augusta would have taken great care over her appearance. She would have had slaves to help her dress and bathe and arrange her hair, as well as do all chores in the household.

BAD TIMES

In Augustus' later years military disasters struck the empire. In AD 6 there was a rebellion in Illyria, and three years later three Roman legions were wiped out in the north of the empire. Augustus, aged 71, became very ill. Julia must have been very worried about these dangers to the Roman Empire and their effect on her husband. Luckily Augustus survived the threats from abroad and the criticisms at home.

Ancient Rome in the time of Agrippina

AFTER THE death of the Emperor Augustus, Rome was a hotbed of murder and intrigue as possible heirs fought for influence and power. Tiberius, the next emperor, left Rome in fear of being assassinated, and he allowed others to rule for him. His successor, Caligula, went mad and survived only four years before he was murdered. The next emperor was Claudius, a man who proved to be a good ruler, but who allowed his wives to continue the murders and intrigues.

Under Claudius, the empire expanded to take in Britain, and many important engineering projects were undertaken, including two aqueducts and a sheltered harbour near Ostia, just outside the city of Rome.

◄ In AD 43 the Emperor Claudius successfully invaded Britain. The Romans completed many building works in Britain, including roads, fortresses and public baths such as the Aquae Sulis baths in Bath, built over natural hot springs.

AGRIPPINA

Emperor's wife
circa AD 15–59

THE VESTAL VIRGINS

In AD 27 Caligula gave his sister Agrippina, and other leading female members of his family, privileges usually only given to special priestesses known as Vestal Virgins. This meant that they were allowed to sit in special seats in the theatre and, unlike other women, to make wills and conduct legal business without the need of a male guardian.

Agrippina was the younger sister of Caligula. The emperor and his sister appear to have had a very stormy relationship, as in AD 40 when Caligula accused his sister of plotting against him and had her banished to a small island.

Caligula was murdered a year later. The next emperor, Claudius, Agrippina's uncle, pardoned her. Agrippina was a very determined person and wanted to be powerful, so she schemed to marry Claudius. Eventually, in AD 49, she got her way and became Empress. She wanted her son from a previous marriage, Nero, adopted as Claudius', heir and so she arranged a marriage between Nero and Claudius' daughter.

◄ Agrippina was an unusually powerful woman for her time. She behaved very much like a man and even wrote her own autobiography.

SPOTLIGHT ON AGRIPPINA

Name:	Julia Agrippina
Born:	AD 15, Ara Ubiorum (modern Cologne)
Died:	AD 59
Family:	Adopted granddaughter of an emperor, sister of an emperor, wife of an emperor, mother of an emperor
Personality:	Deceitful, unforgiving, manipulative
Best moment:	Persuading Claudius to adopt her son Nero as heir
Worst moment:	Being banished to an island by Caligula, thus losing the ability to make her son emperor

Mother of the Emperor

As soon as Agrippina thought that Nero was old enough to take over as emperor, she plotted to have Claudius murdered by feeding him poisoned mushrooms. A year later Claudius' natural son was also poisoned. This meant that, at 16 years of age, Nero became emperor.

For the next few years Agrippina was the most powerful woman in the Roman Empire. She was involved in politics, met foreign ambassadors, and used her powers to get rid of anyone that she didn't like.

► Some historians believe that Nero was mad and that he set fire to Rome to make space to build himself a large palace. It is said that, while the fire raged, he read poetry and played his fiddle.

At first Nero was a good ruler, taking advice from Seneca the poet and philosopher, but as he grew up he became wicked and introduced harsh taxes and laws. He thought he was a great musician (which he wasn't) and made people listen to him for hours on end. Eventually, he began to resent Agrippina's power. He banished her from his house and began to plot her death. His first murder attempt failed, but the second was successful. He sent murderers to her house to beat her to death.

▲ This cameo portrays Agrippina and her husband Claudius (left), and her parents, Germanicus, the popular adopted son of the Emperor Tiberius, and Agrippina the Elder, granddaughter of Augustus (right).

AGRIPPINA'S LUCKY ESCAPE

Nero attempted to murder Agrippina twice. The first time he had a special boat built that would fall apart at a certain signal, and he sent his mother home from a party in it. Unfortunately for him, the boat failed to do the job and Agrippina jumped overboard when she realized that a murder attempt was taking place. She swam ashore and pretended that she thought it was an accident.

Ancient Rome in the time of Hadrian

IN AD 68, Nero killed himself, an event that ended a period of emperors choosing a close relative or adopted son as their heir. Rome then entered a period of chaos as emperor after emperor tried to seize control. During the year after Nero's death, three men in turn became emperor, and each one died by murder or suicide within a few months.

After this, Rome had a relatively peaceful time with emperors who were good for the empire. The Emperor Trajan looked after the poor and saw to the repair of thousands of kilometres of roads, but he spent too much time and money on fighting in the eastern part of the empire.

By AD 117, the empire stretched across most of modern Europe, from Germany and Britain in the north to the coast of north Africa in the south. It took in the entire coast of the Mediterranean, Greece and the modern Balkans, and it extended east into Palestine, Syria and Mesopotamia.

◄ Hadrian's Wall in the north of England was built to prevent the Scots from invading Roman Britain. Other borders were also strengthened at this time. In Germany, for example, strong wooden barriers were put in place along the empire's frontiers.

HADRIAN
Emperor
circa AD 76–138

Hadrian was made emperor in AD 117. He proved himself to be a capable and good ruler of Rome. He followed Augustus Caesar's advice that the empire should not extend beyond the Euphrates river in Mesopotamia. Trajan had conquered Armenia in AD 114 and Mesopotamia in AD 116, but it was too expensive to maintain armies there and Hadrian ordered the withdrawal of Roman troops. He improved the army, strengthened the empire's frontiers and improved conditions for the poor in Rome. He spent ten years of his rule travelling all over the empire, conducting a personal survey on how it was run.

HADRIAN'S WALL

Hadrian visited the north of Britain, where he decided to build a great stone wall, from coast to coast, to keep out raiders from the north. The wall was built around AD 122 and was 117 km long. Twelve garrisons, each made up of hundreds of soldiers, were posted along it. It was built in ten years and lasted until the withdrawal of Roman troops from Britain in AD 410. The wall can still be seen today.

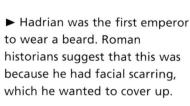

► Hadrian was the first emperor to wear a beard. Roman historians suggest that this was because he had facial scarring, which he wanted to cover up.

SPOTLIGHT ON HADRIAN

Name:	Publius Aelius Hadrianus
Born:	24th January AD 76
Family:	Adopted son of Emperor Trajan, his second cousin
Married:	Vibia Sabina, no children
Personality:	Practical, not entirely honest, gifted but eccentric
Great achievement:	Building a wall across Britain
Worst act:	Causing a war in Jerusalem that killed half a million people

Rebellion in Jerusalem

Hadrian had beautiful buildings erected in almost every city in the empire and renovated several of Rome's earlier monuments. One mistake he made was to build a temple to Jupiter on the site of an important Jewish temple in Jerusalem. This caused a rebellion in AD 132, which lasted three years and caused the death of over a half a million Jews.

▶ After his death, Hadrian was buried three times. Firstly at Baiae where he died, then in the gardens of Domitia in Rome, and, finally, his ashes were buried in the mausoleum he had built for himself.

Even though he was a good ruler, Hadrian was hated by the Roman senators. When he first became emperor, he was blamed for the murders of two senators and, even though he denied having them killed, people mistrusted him. At the end of his life he made some more bad choices about how to secure his successor and he forced two of his own relatives to commit suicide because he thought they opposed his choice of successor. One of these relatives was an old man of 90.

▲ A relief carving showing the Romans stealing objects from the Jewish temple in Jerusalem in AD 70.

ANTINOOS' SACRIFICE

Hadrian had a very close friend; a young man called Antinoos. He took him on his travels in AD 130 and one day, when they were on a boat trip on the Nile in Egypt, Antinoos mysteriously died. Hadrian claimed that he had fallen overboard but some Roman historians suggest that Antinoos killed himself as a sacrifice in some strange religious rite. Hadrian grieved for the loss of his friend, named a new star after him and founded a new city, Antinoopolis, on the spot where he died.

TARQUINSPARTACUSJULIUS CAESARVIRGILJULIA AUGUSTAAGRIPPINA**HADRIAN**MARCUS AURELIUSCONSTANTINE

Ancient Rome in the time of Marcus Aurelius

HADRIAN WAS followed by Antoninus, who ruled for 23 years. He was another emperor who helped the empire by avoiding expensive wars and strengthening its northern borders. In contrast to this period of relative peace, the rule of the next emperor, Marcus Aurelius, was dominated by border wars and a terrible plague that killed thousands of people and lasted over ten years.

▼ The war in Parthia (modern northern Iran) was very successful. Marcus Aurelius celebrated by having his troops march in a triumphal procession into the city.

The Roman Empire at this time consisted of provinces, each one under the leadership of a governor who was closely controlled by the emperor. Great changes were being made all over the empire as citizens in every province were given equal rights with the people of Rome itself. When war broke out, the provincial governors looked to Rome for assistance. The first major war began in Parthia on the eastern frontier of the empire in AD 161, while the second broke out on the northern border when Germanic tribes invaded northern Italy.

Hadrian nominated first Antoninus and then two people, Marcus Aurelius and Lucius Verus, as his heirs.

MARCUS AURELIUS

Emperor circa AD 121–180

Antoninus favoured Marcus Aurelius, who was like a son to him and even married his daughter, Faustina. Marcus Aurelius and Faustina were married for 30 years and had 18 children.

When Antoninus died, both Marcus Aurelius and Lucius Verus wanted his job. In the past this would have led to civil war and assassinations as two sides fought for control, but Marcus Aurelius was a good and practical man and so agreed to rule with Lucius Verus.

Verus was put in charge of the Roman army during its war with Parthia. Although Verus earned a bad reputation for having fun while his generals did all the work, the war went well for Rome. In AD 169, after the death of Verus, a war broke out in the north of the empire. This time, Marcus Aurelius himself went to take charge of the situation and he spent five years fighting a terrible and expensive war.

THE PLAGUE

When the triumphant Roman soldiers arrived back from Parthia in AD 166, carrying the spoils of war, they were also carrying the plague. By the following year this was a major epidemic in Rome. Galen, a famous philosopher and doctor, lived in Rome through the epidemic, and his description of the plague suggests that it was smallpox.

► Marcus Aurelius was a serious and thoughtful man. Even though much of his reign was spent in warfare, he was also known for his philosophical views as contained in his book, *Meditations*.

SPOTLIGHT ON MARCUS AURELIUS

Name:	Marcus Aurelius
Born:	26th April AD 121
Died:	17th March AD 180
Family:	Wealthy Spanish olive oil merchants
Married:	Annia Galeria Faustina, daughter of Emperor Antoninus Pius, May AD 145
Children:	8 sons, 6 daughters, only 6 survived childhood and 5 survived their father
Character:	A serious, hard-working man who avoided all luxuries
Remembered for:	His reforms in Rome and his book of philosophy, the *Meditations*
Famous last words:	'Why weep for me instead of thinking about the plague?'

The Conspiracy against Marcus Aurelius

In AD 175, while Marcus Aurelius was at war, rumours started to circulate that he had been killed. Cassius, the governor of Syria, conspired with Faustina, Marcus' wife, to seize power. He chose what he thought was a loyal army and headed towards Rome, but he was assassinated by his troops before he got there and the revolt ended. Marcus decided not to punish the conspirators, partly because his wife was involved, and partly because he believed that Cassius had not intended personal harm to him.

◄ In AD 176 a column celebrating Marcus Aurelius' victories in war was erected in Rome. It can still be seen there today.

After the revolt, Marcus and Faustina set off to tour the eastern provinces where all the trouble had started. While they were there, Faustina died and, despite the rumours about her part in the conspiracy, Marcus grieved over her death and never remarried. In AD 178 he and his son, Commodus, set off again to put down the invasions along the northern border. He spent the next two years leading his troops in the north and died without returning to Rome and with the war unresolved.

► A bronze statue of Marcus Aurelius on horseback. He spent much of his reign campaigning in the outer regions of the Roman Empire and must have spent a lot of time on horseback.

MARCUS' REFORMS

Throughout all the long wars that Marcus Aurelius had to fight he was also a good ruler and tried to change some of the worst of Rome's laws. He changed the laws of inheritance so that children could inherit from their mother, and tried to reduce the deaths of slaves in the games by using actors in mock battles instead.

Ancient Rome in the time of Constantine

AFTER THE death of Marcus Aurelius, the Roman Empire went through a difficult century or so, during which 29 emperors ruled, most of them selfish men who were quickly assassinated by their rivals. During this time, the army supported whichever candidate offered them the most money. One emperor, Caracalla, even doubled the army's pay to gain their loyalty. Caracalla also passed a law that made everyone in the empire a citizen. This meant that they were all under the same legal system, and this gave the empire more unity.

However, the empire became more and more unstable as the threats from around the borders increased. One emperor, Valerian, who was captured by the King of Persia (modern Iran), remained a prisoner for the rest of his life. Another emperor, Diocletian, divided the empire up and created two chief emperors and two more deputy emperors. This often caused more problems, with the four emperors fighting for control.

► Sol, the sun god. This was one of the many gods worshipped by the Romans before the arrival of Christianity in the fourth century.

CONSTANTINE
Soldier and Emperor
circa AD 272–337

CONSTANTINE'S CONVERSION

As Constantine was about to attack Rome in AD 312, he saw a vision in the sky of a cross of light and the words 'Conquer by this'. That night in his dreams, Christ appeared to him and instructed him to carry a banner with a Christian symbol into all his battles. The next day he won an important battle. From that day he became a Christian.

Constantine was the son of Constantius, one of the four emperors created by Diocletian. Like his father, he was a good and talented soldier. When Constantius died in AD 306, civil war broke out between the remaining emperors, until, in AD 312, Constantine invaded Italy and was proclaimed emperor in Rome.

For a time he ruled only half the empire, but, in AD 324, war broke out between him and the emperor of the east. Constantine was victorious and took control of the entire empire.

◄ Constantine afer his conversion to Christianity. His staff carries the symbols of Christianity, made up of the Greek letter 'chi' (X) and 'rho' (P).

SPOTLIGHT ON CONSTANTINE

Name:	Gaius Flavius Valerius Constantinus Nobilissimus Caesar
Born:	27th February AD 272, Naissus
Died:	22nd May AD 337, near Nicomedia (modern Turkey)
Family:	Son of Constantius Chlorus, the Senior Emperor of the West
Married:	1. Minervina 2. Fausta
Children:	4 sons, 2 daughters
Character:	A man of sound judgement, well educated
Best moment:	Seeing a vision of a shining cross
Worst moment:	The execution of his son Crispus for adultery
Famous for:	Giving official support to Christianity in the Empire, and establishing Constantinople

Creation of Constantinople

Once in power, Constantine thought it was important to move the capital of the empire away from Rome. It was threatened by border invasions from all sides and it was also a pagan city, full of temples to the old gods. He built a new city that was named Constantinople (modern Istanbul) and he commissioned a huge building programme to make it into his capital.

► The Arch of Constantine in Rome, celebrating Constantine's military triumphs.

Constantine also reorganized the army and disbanded the Praetorian Guard, who had over the years taken countless bribes from candidates for the job of emperor. He brought in new taxes, new laws based on Christian values and in his later years conducted several border wars, making the empire safer from an attack from outside. His worst mistake, though, was to divide up the empire again, between his three sons and his nephew, which created new problems.

▼ A 13th-century wall painting showing Constantine (in the middle) leading Pope Sylvester I (riding on horseback) into Rome. As a follower of Christianity, he built many churches in Rome.

CONSTANTINE'S HARSH ACTS

Although Constantine is known as a good ruler and the first Christian ruler of any country, he was capable of acting very harshly. In AD 325, he had a rival emperor, Licinus, murdered, along with his nine-year-old son, and the next year another rival emperor was killed. In AD 326, he had his own eldest son, Crispus, executed for adultery, and he later drove his own wife to suicide for falsely accusing his son.

The end of the Empire

AFTER CONSTANTINE'S death in AD 337, the empire experienced a terrible civil war. By the end of the fourth century AD, the eastern and western parts of the empire were completely separate.

The fourth and fifth centuries saw huge migrations of people across what is now modern Russia, the Balkans, Germany and France. One tribe would move westwards, displacing another tribe and sending them further west, until eventually a tribe called the Vandals swept into Gaul and Spain and into north Africa, areas of which had been part of the Roman Empire for centuries. At the same time a group of tribes, the Goths, invaded Italy itself. Britain was abandoned as Roman troops fell back to Rome's defence. But it was too late.

▼ Justinian (527–565), the last great emperor of Constantinople, retook part of the western empire from the Goths, but at an enormous cost.

In AD 410 Rome itself was invaded by Alaric the Goth and in AD 476, the western emperor was deposed and Italy taken over by the Goths.

Although Constantinople continued as the capital of the eastern empire, ruled over by Latin-speaking emperors, there was no connection with the old empire after the rule of the emperor Justinian in the sixth century. In the tenth century, the eastern church split with the church of Rome, and, in the 15th century, Constantinople itself was taken by the Turks.

What is amazing about the Roman Empire is not its collapse but the fact that it lasted so long and grew so big, at a time when it took months to cross from one end of the empire to the other. Its legacy to us is enormous. Our modern alphabet is Roman, as are the alphabets of Italy, France, Portugal, Spain, Germany, Scandinavia and many other countries. Our calendar was invented by the Romans and many modern laws are based on those of Rome. The dome, cement, the postal service, flushing toilets, central heating, the fire service, hospitals, glass windows and social security payments were all invented by the Romans.

▲ The Pont du Gard near Avignon in France. Built by the Romans in the second century AD, this is a remarkable feat of engineering. It carried water along a channel carried on three arches, 50 metres above the river.

Timeline

BC

753	Founding of Rome; rule of the seven kings begins
510	Expulsion of Tarquin from Rome
509	The Roman Republic established
201	Defeat of Carthaginians; Rome becomes the most important country in the Mediterranean
100	Birth of Julius Caesar
73–71	Revolt of Spartacus
71	Death of Spartacus
70	Birth of Virgil
59	First consulship of Julius Caesar
58–50	Julius Caesar's wars in Gaul
57	Birth of Livia (Julia Augusta)
49	Julius Caesar becomes the most powerful man in Rome
44	Julius Caesar assassinated
43	First consulship of Augustus
27	Augustus becomes the sole ruler of Rome
27–19	Virgil writes the *Aeneid*
19	Death of Virgil

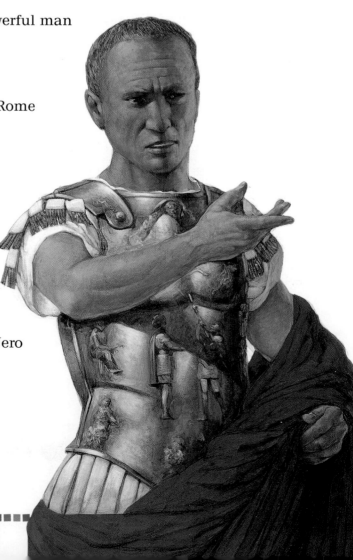

AD

14	Death of Augustus
15	Birth of Agrippina
29	Death of Livia (Julia Augusta)
c30	Crucifixion of Jesus
37	Birth of Nero
49	Agrippina marries Claudius
54	Claudius is poisoned; accession of Nero
59	Nero has Agrippina murdered
68	Death of Nero
76	Birth of Hadrian
117	Hadrian becomes emperor
121	Birth of Marcus Aurelius
127	Hadrian's Wall completed

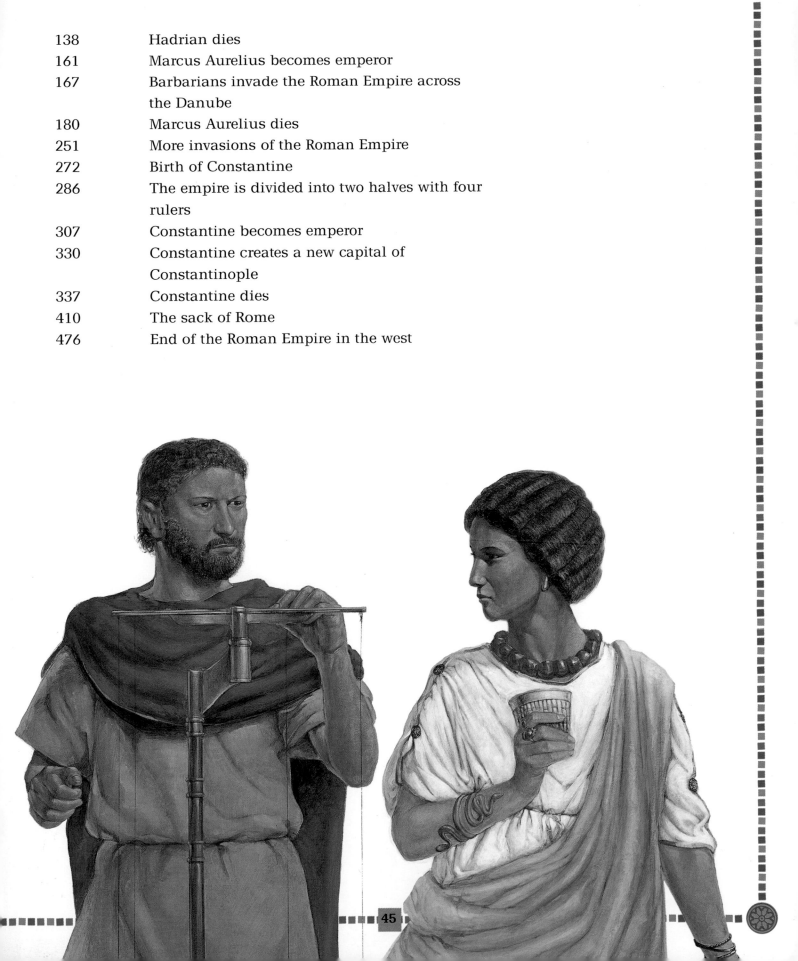

Glossary

absolute ruler   A ruler who has no limits to his power

aqueduct   A manmade channel to transport water over long distances

banish   Send someone away from their country as a punishment

booty   Goods taken from defeated enemies in war

circa   Used before a date to mean 'about' or 'approximately'

citizen   A person who lived in Rome or one of the colonies and who was subject to Roman law, had the right of marriage, and, in some cases, could vote in elections.

city state   A self-governing city not under the rule of a bigger government

conscripted   Forced into service in the army

Etruscans   An early civilization based in Italy

Gaul   An area of Europe roughly covering modern France

Latins   The people who inhabited central Italy

legacy   Something handed down from the past

legion   A division of the Roman army with about 5,000 soldiers, made up of foot soldiers and cavalry

mausoleum   A building that houses a tomb or tombs

myth   A story, often made up, to explain some events in the past

praetorian guard   The emperor's bodyguard, usually 10 cohorts of 1,000 men each

prestige   Other people's respect for your accomplishments

prophecy   A story that predicts the future

provincial governor   The person in charge of a country defeated and then run by the Roman Empire

republic   A system of government where elected people (in Rome's case just men) govern the country

senate   A council of around 600 nobles who advised the king or emperor and helped to govern the country

sybil   A priestess who could foretell the future

tyrant   A single, often cruel, ruler who rules by force of arms

Further information

Websites

http://www.julen.net/aw/
This is the Ancient World Web site. You can search it for particular topics on ancient Rome

http://ancienthistory.miningco.com/msubjulio.htm
Pictures of ancient Roman sites, portraits of the emperors, access to a chat line and lots more.

http://members.aol.com/Donnclass/Romelife.html
Educational material on ancient Rome with useful links to other sites

Books to read

A Roman Town by Jonathon Rutland (Hutchinson & Co, 1977)
Ancient Rome (Eyewitness Guides) by Simon James (Dorling Kindersley, 1990)
Growing Up in Ancient Rome by Mike Corbishley (Eagle Books, 1993)
The Ancient World: Rome by Pat Levy and Sean Sheehan (Wayland, 1998)
The Roman News by Andrew Langley and Philip de Souza (Walker Books, 1996)

Places to Visit

Vindolanda – an excavated fort close to Hadrian's Wall
The British Museum – lots of artefacts from ancient Rome and Roman Britain
Pompei – the extensive remains of a Roman town in Italy, which was buried under volcanic ash from the sudden eruption of Mount Vesuvius

Index